Collins

easy learning

Problem solving and reasoning

Ages 7–9

Rachel Axten-Higgs

How to use this book

- Find a quiet, comfortable place to work, away from other distractions.
- Make sure your child has plenty of paper to write their ideas and working on.
- This book takes a thematic approach to problem solving and reasoning.
- Tackle one theme at a time.
- Within each theme there are lots of problem-solving and reasoning activities for your child to complete. Your child will have to select and apply the appropriate number, measurement and / or geometry skills to solve each problem.
- Help with reading the instructions where necessary, and ensure that your child understands what to do.
- If your child is struggling with a particular activity, discuss with them what they know, what they need to find out and how they might go about it. If your child is still struggling, leave the activity and return to it when you know they are likely to achieve it.
- Help and encourage your child to check their own answers as they complete each theme.
- Discuss with your child what they have learnt.
- Let your child return to their favourite pages once they have been completed, to talk about the activities.
- Reward your child with plenty of praise and encouragement.

Special features

- Yellow boxes: introduce each theme.
- Orange boxes: contain different problem-solving and reasoning activities based on the theme.
- Orange shaded boxes: offer advice to parents on how to support their child's learning.

ACKNOWLEDGEMENTS

Published by Collins
An imprint of HarperCollins*Publishers*
1 London Bridge Street
London SE1 9GF

© HarperCollins*Publishers* Limited 2018

ISBN 9780008275365

10 9 8 7 6 5 4

All images and illustrations are
© Shutterstock.com and
© HarperCollins*Publishers*

All rights reserved. No part of this publication may be reproduced, stored in a retrieval system, or transmitted, in any form or by any means, electronic, mechanical, photocopying, recording or otherwise, without the prior permission of Collins.

British Library Cataloguing in Publication Data

A Catalogue record for this publication is available from the British Library

Author: Rachel Axten-Higgs
Commissioning editor: Michelle I'Anson
Editor and project manager: Rebecca Skinner
Cover design: Sarah Duxbury
Interior concept design: Ian Wrigley
Page layouts: Q2A Media Services PVT Ltd.
Production: Lyndsey Rogers
Printed by Bell and Bain Ltd, Glasgow

MIX
Paper from
responsible source
FSC™ C007454
www.fsc.org

This book is produced from independently certified FSC™ paper to ensure responsible forest management.

For more information visit:
www.harpercollins.co.uk/green

Contents

Going shopping

You are food shopping with your parents and brother.
If you are helpful, you will be given £1 to spend on something you choose.

1 Your mum sends you to the home baking section.
She asks you to bring back the heaviest bag of plain flour that you can find.
Here are the packets of plain flour that are on the shelf:

2 kg   1500 g   1.75 kg   1000 g   1 kg   2500 g

      ✓

Tick (✓) the heaviest bag of flour.

2 You need 200 g of bananas.
Packets of bananas cost 96p for 200 g.
Loose bananas cost 45p for 100 g.

Is it cheaper to buy a packet or loose bananas?   packet 96 / 96p ✓   loose 90 ✓

How much money do you save? 6p P ✓

3 You and your brother can choose two boxes of cereal.
You pick a box of Wheat Puffs, which costs £1.67
Your brother picks a box of Coco Munch, which costs £2.09

How much do your parents spend on cereal in total? £ 3.76 ✓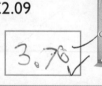

When shopping with your child, encourage them to look at the different shapes and sizes of packets and the quantities and weights. This will help them become aware of the use of measurements in real-life terms.

4 You need to buy a ball of string for a school project.
You need 157 cm for your project.

80 cm	1.10 m	1.5 m	120 cm	200 cm
☐	☐	☑	☐	☐

Tick (✓) the ball that you need to buy to have enough string for your project.

Your dad says he needs one and a half metres of string for the garden.

Which ball of string is equal to one and a half metres? _____

5 Your brother is fed up with how long the shopping is taking.
He says, "We've been here for an hour already!"
You arrived at 09:23 am and it is now 10:18 am.

Is your brother correct?   yes ☐   no ☑

Explain your answer.

Because its 09:23 am and 10:18   18 + 23 = 41

6 You are given £1 for helping.
You want to buy the sweets that are the best value for money.

99p for 150 g	£1 for 100 g	98p for 125 g	98p for 100 g
Chocolate mice	Strawberry laces	Jelly beans	Pick and mix

Circle the option that is the best value for money.

Explain your answer.

100 g £1 For Strawberry lacy

Planning a party

You are planning a party for your birthday.
You can choose the theme.

What theme have you chosen? ___frozen___ ✓

1 You have invited 29 friends to your party.
8 friends cannot come.
One friend has asked if she can bring her 2 brothers and you have agreed.

How many children will be at the party? (Don't forget yourself!) | 23 | ✓ children

2 You want to buy themed plates for the party.
Plates are sold in packs of 8.
You need 1 plate for each child.

How many packs do you need to buy? | 3 | ✓ packs

Packs of plates cost £1.49 each.

What will be the total cost of the packs of plates you need to buy? £ | 4.47 | ✓

3 Each child at your party will get a party bag
You will get lots of presents, so you do not need a party bag.
You have found some balls to put in the party bags.
The balls are sold in packs of 3. You need 1 ball for each bag.

How many packs of balls do you need to buy? | 8 | ✓ packs

How many balls will you have left over? | 1 | ✓ ball

Include your child when planning real-life events so they learn that maths is important in everyday life. For example, when buying party tableware, tell them how many people are coming and ask them to work out how many packs of each item are needed. You could extend this further by asking them to work out the cost.

4 You will give each child at the party a bottle of water.
Water bottles are sold in packs of 4.

How many packs will you need to buy? [6] packs

Each bottle of water holds 250 ml.

How many ml of water do you get in a pack of 4 bottles? [ ] ml

5 Your party is at the village hall.
The village hall has tables that seat 8 people.

How many tables will you need to seat all the children? [ ] tables

How many empty spaces will there be at the tables? [ ] empty spaces

6 The village hall has 42 chairs.
They are stored as stacks of 6 chairs.
Water has dripped through the roof and ruined 3 stacks of chairs.

How many chairs have been ruined altogether? [ ] chairs

Are there enough chairs left for you and all your guests?

yes [ ]   no [ ]

Show your working.

_____

_____

7 You have hired the village hall from 9:30 am until 2:00 pm.
Your party starts at 10:30 am and lasts for 2 hours.

How long do you have to set up before the party? ☐ 1 ☐ hour

How long do you have to tidy up after the party? ☐ 2 ☐ hours

How long have you hired the hall for in total? ☐ 5 ☐ hours

It costs £10 an hour to hire the hall (£5 for half an hour).

What is the total cost of hiring the hall for your party? £ ☐ 20.5 ☐

8 There will be a face painter at your party.
The face painter charges £2 per face.

If 18 children have their faces painted,

what will the cost be? £ ☐

It takes the face painter 5 minutes to paint one face.

How long would it take to paint 18 faces?
Give your answer in hours and minutes.

☐ hour ☐ minutes

9 A magician is coming to the party.
The magician charges £4 per child.

What is the total cost for the magician? £ ☐

Your parents have been given a voucher for £10 off the cost
of the magician.

If they use the voucher, how much do they need to pay the magician? £ ☐

10 There are going to be party games, so you need to buy some prizes.
There are 4 games, and 2 prizes are needed for each game.

How many prizes do you need to buy? ⬚ prizes

Your mum says you can spend £4 on the prizes.

How much do you have to spend on each prize? ⬚ p

You want to buy pots of bubbles for the prizes.

£2.49 **1 litre**   79p **250 ml**   65p **200 ml**   49p **150 ml**   55p **rainbow**   70p **touchable**

⬚ ⬚ ⬚ ⬚ ⬚ ⬚

Tick (✓) the bubbles can you afford to buy.

11 You are having a piñata at your party.
You have £5 to spend on the prizes to put in it.

Here are the prizes you can choose from and the price for one item.

2p   6p   5p   7p   4p   3p   8p

⬚ ⬚ ⬚ ⬚ ⬚ ⬚ ⬚

The prizes are sold in sets of 100.
Tick (✓) all the prizes you could afford to buy a set of.

Which set of prizes will leave you with the most change from £5? _____

Explain your answer.

_____

_____

Going camping

You are going camping in a tent with your parents.

1 When you arrive at the campsite, you help your parents set up the tent.
The instructions include a diagram of the floor of the tent.
There are measurements on the diagram.

Calculate the perimeter of the floor of the tent in centimetres. [ ] cm

Your dad says, "The floor of the tent is symmetrical."

Draw a line of symmetry on the diagram to show this.

Is the front of the porch perpendicular or parallel to the living area?

perpendicular [ ] parallel [ ]

2 Your parents paid £28.50 in total for you all to stay on the campsite.
They think they paid too much money.

Your family has 2 adults and 1 child.
It is a 3-person tent.
You are staying for 2 nights.

Look at the tariff card and work out how much your parents should have paid.

TARIFF CARD

1 person tent	£4.00 per night
2–3 person tent	£7.50 per night
4 person tent or larger	£10.00 per night
Each adult	£2.00 per night
Each child	£1.50 per night

£ [ ]

How much extra have your parents paid? £ [ ]

---

3 It is 3:30 pm.
A blackboard shows the following activities:

> Archery – 6:00 pm (sessions last 30 minutes)
>
> Golf – available from 9:30 am to 5:00 pm (allow 40 minutes to complete)
>
> Tractor Rides – 2:00 pm, 4:20 pm and 6:40 pm (rides last 20 minutes)

Do you have time to play golf before the next tractor ride?   yes [ ]   no [ ]

Show your working.

_____

_____

If you do archery, will you be finished in time for the last tractor ride of the day?

yes [ ]   no [ ]

Show your working.

_____

_____

Decorating a bedroom

Your parents have said that you can redecorate your bedroom.
You need to think about new furniture, a carpet and wall decorations.

1 You decide that you want to paint one wall of your bedroom.
The following diagram shows you how big the wall is.

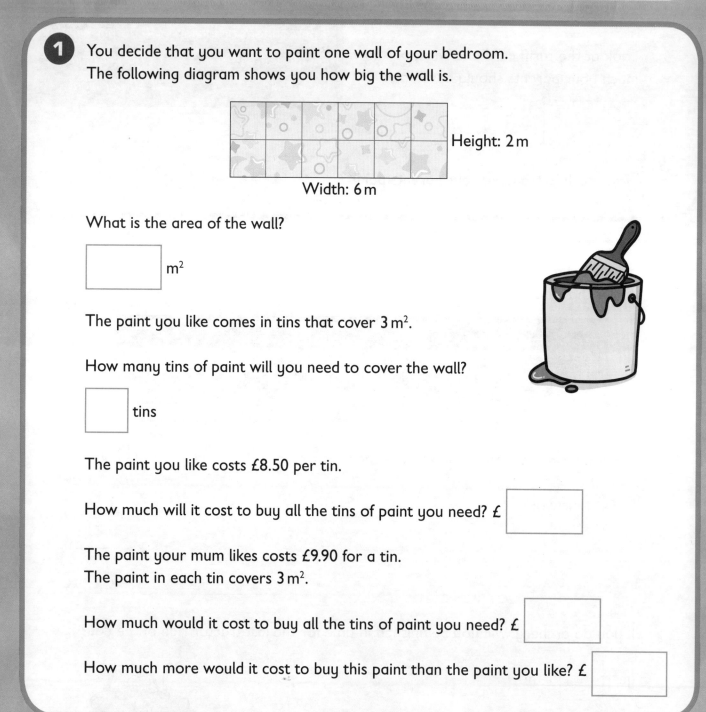

Height: 2 m

Width: 6 m

What is the area of the wall?

[   ] m²

The paint you like comes in tins that cover 3 m².

How many tins of paint will you need to cover the wall?

[   ] tins

The paint you like costs £8.50 per tin.

How much will it cost to buy all the tins of paint you need? £ [   ]

The paint your mum likes costs £9.90 for a tin.
The paint in each tin covers 3 m².

How much would it cost to buy all the tins of paint you need? £ [   ]

How much more would it cost to buy this paint than the paint you like? £ [   ]

In this topic, your child is asked to find the area of various parts of the bedroom. Calculating the area of a rectangle uses a simple formula (length × width). However, at this stage children are expected to find the area by counting squares. This helps them gain an understanding of what area is. Measurements of area are given in square metres (m²).

2 You choose some items of furniture from a catalogue:

	single bed	£85
	bedside table	£25
	wardrobe	£45
	desk	£35
	chair	£25
	bookcase	£45

What is the total cost of all the items you have chosen?

£ [ ]

Your parents have given you a budget of £225 for furniture.

How much over budget is your list?

£ [ ]

Tick (✓) one item that could be removed from your list so that the total cost exactly matches the budget.

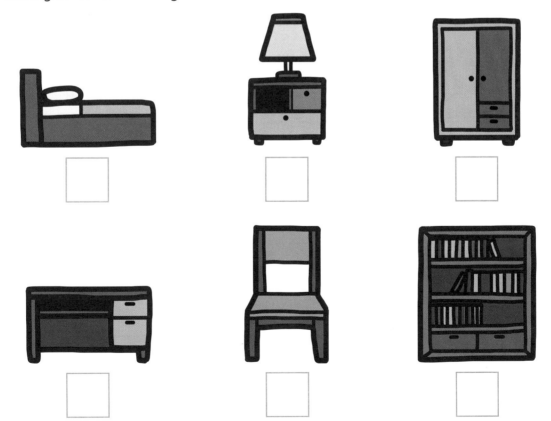

3 You want to know how much free space you will have in your room after all the new furniture is in place.

Here is a floor plan of the room:

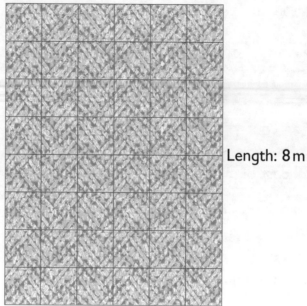

Length: 8 m

Width: 6 m

Find the area of the bedroom floor.

☐ m²

Your parents increase your budget so you can buy all the furniture you chose. You make a list showing the area that each item will take up:

single bed	2 m²
bedside table	0.5 m²
wardrobe	2 m²
desk	2 m²
chair	0.5 m²
bookcase	1 m²

Work out the area that will be left over when all the furniture is in the room.

☐ m²

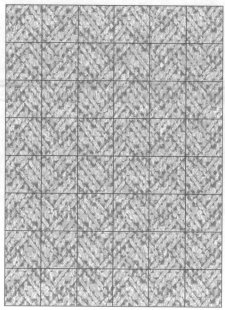

m²

4 Your parents say that you can have a new carpet.
The carpet you like costs £6.00 per m².

What would the total cost of this carpet be?
Use the area that you found in Box 3.

£

The budget for the new carpet is £250.

How much over budget is the carpet you like?

£

You have another look at the carpets.
Here is a price list showing the costs of different carpets per m².

CARPET WAREHOUSE	
checkerboard	£7.00 per m²
plain deep pile (any colour)	£5.00 per m²
plain short pile (any colour)	£4.00 per m²
two-tone deep pile (any 2 colours)	£6.00 per m²
two-tone short pile (any 2 colours)	£5.00 per m²

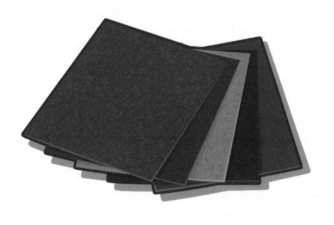

List the carpets that your budget of £250 can buy.

_____

_____

Visiting a library

You go to your local library to borrow a book.

1 You are allowed to borrow a book for 3 weeks.

How many days is this? ☐ days

You borrow a book on 2nd January.

On what date must the book be returned? _____

2 Here are the numbers of books on six different shelves in the library.

Round each number of books to the nearest ten.

Shelf 1: 57 books ☐ to the nearest ten

Shelf 2: 62 books ☐ to the nearest ten

Shelf 3: 89 books ☐ to the nearest ten

Shelf 4: 75 books ☐ to the nearest ten

Shelf 5: 109 books ☐ to the nearest ten

Shelf 6: 155 books ☐ to the nearest ten

What is the total number of books on the six bookshelves? ☐ books

What is the total rounded to the nearest ten? ☐ books

What is the total rounded to the nearest hundred? ☐ books

On the next page, your child will be given two measurements (length and width) for a rectangular book and asked to find the perimeter – the distance all the way around the outside of the rectangle. They may need some help to see that they must add *two* lengths and *two* widths to find the total perimeter.

16

3 Here are the lengths and widths of five different books in the library:

15 cm
8 cm
[ ] cm

24 cm
11 cm
[ ] cm

18 cm
12 cm
[ ] cm

19 cm
13 cm
[ ] cm

24 cm
9 cm
[ ] cm

Calculate the perimeter of each book.

4 The table below shows the number of pages in five different books:

Book	Number of pages	To the nearest ten	To the nearest hundred
1	109		
2	356		
3	274		
4	351		
5	101		

Round each number of pages to the nearest ten and to the nearest hundred to complete the table.

What is the total number of pages in the five books? [ ] pages

What is the total rounded: to the nearest ten? [ ] pages

to the nearest hundred? [ ] pages

to the nearest thousand? [ ] pages

Flying on holiday

Airports are busy places.
Thousands of passengers pass through them every day (especially in August).
You are going to the airport to head off on your summer holidays.

1 Your flight is at 15:45.
You need to check in at the airport 2 hours before that time.

What time do you need to check in?
Write your answer in words as a 12-hour time.

_____

You need to leave home $1\frac{3}{4}$ hours before your check-in time.

What time do you need to leave home?
Write your answer as a 24-hour digital time.

2 You booked your flight online.
On the website there was a diagram of the plane.
There are 6 seats in each row:
3 on each side of the central gangway.
The rows are labelled with letters from A to V.

How many passengers can fit on the plane?

[_____] passengers

The airline you are travelling with has 9 planes leaving the airport today.
They all hold the same number of passengers and are fully booked.

How many passengers will the airline fly out of the airport today?

[_____] passengers

3 In total, 132 suitcases have been checked in to go on 11 planes.
All the planes carry the same number of suitcases.

How many suitcases will be loaded on to each plane? ☐ suitcases

Your hand luggage cannot be more than 10 kg in weight.
The scales show that your backpack weighs 9307 g.

How much more weight could you have in your backpack? ☐ g

4 You pass through airport security.
Your parents are asked how many days you will be staying at your destination.
You will be staying for 2 weeks and 3 days.

How many days is this in total? ☐ days

5 You see a sign that shows how many flights left the airport in July.

**City Airport
July Departures**

Charter flights	= 990
Scheduled international flights	= 4,538
Scheduled domestic flights	= 890

How many scheduled international and domestic flights left the airport in July?

☐ flights

How many flights left the airport in total in July? ☐ flights

Your child could use multiplication to solve the questions in Box 2. When your child is doing more complicated multiplication problems like these, they should use a formal written method that they have been taught at school. Make sure they are able to explain it to you. Do not try to show them an alternative method as this may confuse them!

6 Your family buys lunch in a restaurant at the airport. Here is the menu available:

Menu

Pizza	£7.99
Pasta	£7.49
Main salad	£6.89
Side salad	£3.15
Fries	£3.67
Onion rings	£3.50
Soft drinks	£1.99 (unlimited refills)
Ice-cream	£2.49
Fruit bowl	£2.25

Your family orders 3 pizzas, 1 main salad, 2 portions of fries, 1 portion of onion rings and 4 soft drinks.

How much does this cost altogether? £

For dessert, your family orders 3 ice-creams and 1 fruit bowl.

How much does dessert cost altogether? £

Your parents have a voucher that allows you to buy all your food and drinks for $\frac{1}{2}$ price.

How much is the bill for the whole meal after the voucher has been used?

£

7 On the plane, the flight attendants bring snacks.
Every passenger gets one snack.
The attendants give out 114 standard snacks, 12 vegetarian
snacks and 6 gluten-free snacks

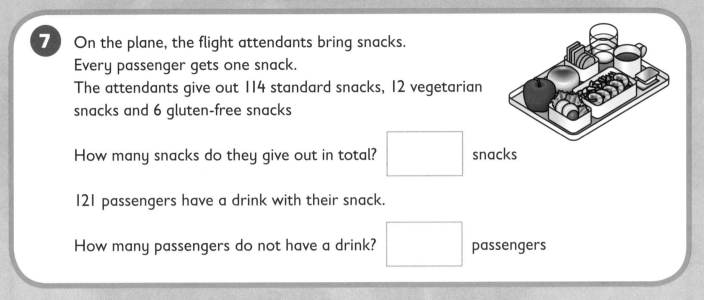

How many snacks do they give out in total? _____ snacks

121 passengers have a drink with their snack.

How many passengers do not have a drink? _____ passengers

8 The plane reaches its highest point in the sky.
The pilot announces that the temperature outside the plane is −55 °C.
The temperature at your destination is 30° C.

What is the temperature difference?

_____ °C

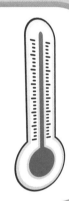

9 Your flight left at 15:45
It takes $2\frac{1}{2}$ hours.

What time do you arrive at your destination?
Write your answer in words as a 12-hour time.

_____

The local time at your destination is 1 hour behind GMT (the time in the UK).

What is the local time at your destination when you arrive?
Write your answer as a 24-hour digital time.

_____

Talk to your child about clocks and times when you are out and about. Test them by asking them what the 12-hour time
is and what the 24-hour time is. Ask them to work out what time you need to leave, by telling them the time you need
to arrive and how long it will take to get there. This is a practical way of helping your child understand time.

Going swimming

You are going swimming at the local pool with a group of friends.

1 As you enter the building, there is a plan on the wall.
The plan shows the volume of water in each of the three swimming pools.

| Learner pool 8,400 litres | Main pool 9,770 litres | Diving pool 9,999 litres |

What is the difference between the volumes of the learner pool and the main pool?

[ ] litres

What is the difference between the volumes of the learner pool and the diving pool?

[ ] litres

What is the total volume of all three pools?

[ ] litres

2 There are 6 of you in your group and you are all juniors.

What is the total cost for your group to swim? £ [ ]

Ajay and Su are members of the swimming club.

Recalculate the total cost for your group. £ [ ]

Adult swim	£3.75
Junior swim	£2.65
Infant swim	£1.50
Swim club member	£1.25

Discuss the idea of 'volume' with your child. Because the word has a mathematical meaning (the amount of liquid or gas within a container) and a more common meaning (how loud something is), children can get confused. It is good to share your experiences of this kind of misunderstanding.

3 You and your friends decide to have a race.
You time how long it takes to swim one length of the main pool.
Here are the results:

You:	34.3 seconds	[ ] to the nearest second
Daniel:	28.8 seconds	[ ] to the nearest second
Ajay:	38.4 seconds	[ ] to the nearest second
Su:	28.2 seconds	[ ] to the nearest second
Anita:	40.5 seconds	[ ] to the nearest second
Sam:	28.9 seconds	[ ] to the nearest second

Who is the fastest? _____

Who is the slowest? _____

Round all the times to the nearest second (whole number).

Using your rounded numbers, work out the total of all the times added together.
Give your answer in minutes and seconds.

[ ] minutes [ ] seconds

4 The lifeguards carry out a head count every 30 minutes.
The total number allowed in the three pools altogether is 150 people.

At 15:00 there are 60 people in the main pool, 54 people in the learner pool and 10 people in the diving pool.

How many more people can enter the pools? [ ] people

34 people get out and 12 people get in.

How many people are in the pools in total now? [ ] people

Pizza takeaway

You have some friends over on Friday evening to watch a film.
You order takeaway pizzas to be delivered.

1 Here is the takeaway menu:

	Small	Medium	Large
Pizzas			
Cheese and tomato	£4.99	£6.99	£8.99
Seafood	£5.49	£7.49	£9.49
Chicken and mushroom	£5.49	£7.49	£9.49
Four cheeses	£5.99	£7.99	£9.99
Meat feast	£5.99	£7.99	£9.99
Veggie	£5.59	£7.59	£9.59

Sides		**Drinks**	
Potato wedges	£2.49	Cola	£1.99
Garlic bread	£3.49	Lemonade	£1.49
Dough balls	£3.99		

You and your friends order 1 medium cheese and tomato pizza, 1 large chicken and mushroom pizza, 1 large veggie pizza, 2 portions of potato wedges, 1 garlic bread and 1 bottle of cola.

What is the total cost of your order? £ ⬚

There are 5 of you (including you), and you each have £10.

How much change will there be from your pizza order? £ ⬚

To have your order delivered costs £3.47 extra.

How much change will there be after this is cost added to your bill? £ ⬚

You split the change equally between you.

How much change do you each get? £ ⬚

2 When your pizzas arrive, they are already cut into slices
The medium pizza is cut into 8 equal slices.
The large pizzas are each cut into 12 equal slices.
All of your friends take some pizza.

 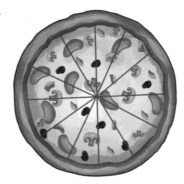 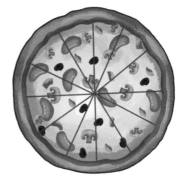

You look at the large chicken and mushroom pizza.

Daisy has taken $\frac{1}{4}$ of the pizza.

Steve has taken 1 slice.
Ajay has taken 2 slices.
Su has taken 3 slices.

How much chicken and mushroom pizza is left?
Express your answer as a fraction.

You look at the medium cheese and tomato pizza.

There is $\frac{3}{8}$ remaining.

How many slices have been taken? [ ] slices

You look at the large veggie pizza.

Steve has taken $\frac{1}{4}$ of this pizza.

Ajay has taken $\frac{1}{12}$.

How many slices of pizza are left? [ ] slices

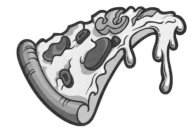

You take 1 slice of each pizza and no one takes any more.

What fraction of each pizza is left?

Chicken and mushroom: [ ]   Cheese and tomato: [ ]   Veggie: [ ]

When serving food, ask your child to help you share amounts equally between people. This is a practical way to help strengthen their understanding of division and fractions.

3 The pizzas are all in square boxes
One pizza fits into each box exactly.
The medium pizza has a diameter of 30 cm.
The large pizzas each have a diameter of 45 cm.

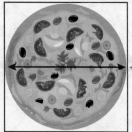

The diameter is the distance across a circle from one side to the other, going through the exact centre.

What is the perimeter of the medium box:

in centimetres? [ ] cm

in metres as a decimal fraction? [ ] m

What is the perimeter of a large box:

in centimetres? [ ] cm

in metres as a decimal fraction? [ ] m

---

4 The garlic bread is rectangular and flat.
It is cut into 15 pieces.

How many pieces will each person get if you share it out equally? [ ] pieces

Ajay does not want any garlic bread, so only 4 of you are sharing it.
You share it out so that each person gets the same number of whole pieces.

How many pieces are left over? [ ] pieces

You cut each of the left-over pieces of garlic bread into 4.

How many smaller pieces do you have? [ ] pieces

You share the smaller pieces evenly between the 4 of you.

How many small pieces do you each get? [ ] pieces

5 Your mum points out to you that it would have been cheaper to buy pizza from a supermarket and cook it at home.

She shows you the supermarket prices online.

	Supermarket price	Takeaway price
Medium cheese and tomato pizza	£3.99	£4.99
Large chicken and mushroom pizza	£4.99	£9.49
Large veggie pizza	£4.99	£9.59

What is the total cost for the three pizzas from the takeaway?

£

What is the total cost for the three pizzas from the supermarket?

£

What is the total difference in price?

£

6 You ordered 2 portions of potato wedges.
Each portion contained 25 wedges.
You share the wedges equally between the 5 of you.

How many wedges does each person get?

 wedges

Olympic Games

You are watching the Olympic Games on television.
The Olympic Games only takes place once every four years.

1 The commentator gives you information about each country.
He tells you that there are 207 countries taking part in the games.
119 of them are in the northern hemisphere.

How many of the countries are **not** from the northern hemisphere?

[ ] countries

2 You watch the heptathlon.
Each athlete must compete in seven different events.
The points scored in the different events are added together.
After Day 1, the athletes have the following points:

Athlete	Points
USA	82
Russia	81
China	76
Kenya	57
Ukraine	54
Great Britain	45
Slovakia	19

What is the difference between the highest score and the lowest score?

[ ] points

What is the combined total of USA, Russia and China? points

What is the lowest number of points that Great Britain needs to overtake the USA?

[ ] points

How many points have been scored in total? [ ] points

3 It is Day 2 of the heptathlon.
The points table now looks like this:

Athlete	Points
Russia	156
Great Britain	137
USA	125
China	97
Slovakia	89
Kenya	72
Ukraine	69

How many points has Ukraine scored since Day 1?

[ ] points

How many points has Great Britain scored since Day 1?

[ ] points

What is the total of all the points scored so far?

[ ] points

What is the lowest number of points that Great Britain needs to overtake Russia?

[ ] points

4 Below are the four longest distances thrown in the men's shot put final:
21.03 m   20.29 m   21.15 m   21.36 m

Put the distances in order, from shortest to longest.

_____

The current world record is 22.84 m.

What is the difference between the longest distance thrown in the final and the world record?

[ ] m

5 The swimming events take place in a new stadium.
The new stadium can seat ten thousand, five hundred spectators.

Complete the pictogram to show this information.

🧍	
🧍	
🧍	
🧍	
🧍	
🧍	
🧍	

Old stadium   **New stadium**

Key

🧍 1,000 spectators

🧍 500 spectators

How many more spectators can be seated in the new stadium than the old stadium?

spectators

There are spectators in half the seats in the new swimming stadium.

How many spectators is this? | | spectators

Another 2,500 spectators arrive.

How many more spectators could be seated in the stadium now? | | spectators

6 You watch the 100 metres sprint race.
The results are shown below:

Athlete	Time in seconds
South Africa	9.94
USA	9.89
Jamaica 1	9.81
Jamaica 2	9.93
Canada	9.91

Which athlete had the fastest time?

_____

Which athlete had the slowest time?

_____

Write the athletes in order, starting with the slowest.

_____

7 At the end of the Olympic Games, the number of gold medals won by each country is shown in a graph:

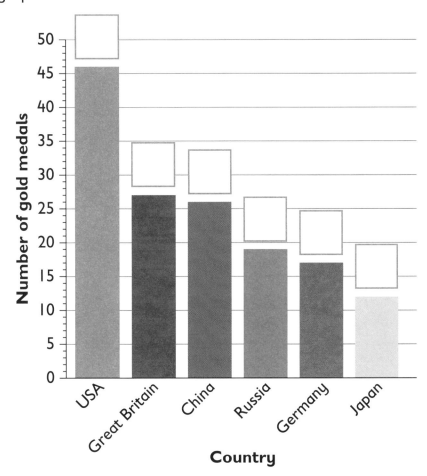

Write the number of medals that each country won in the boxes on the graph.

Which country won the most gold medals? _____

Answers

Page 4
Going shopping
1. 2500 g
2. loose
   6p
3. £3.76

Page 5
4. 200 cm
   1.5 m (accept: the green one)
5. no
   It has only been 55 minutes (so not quite an hour).
6. Chocolate mice
   You get the greatest weight for the least amount of money. Also accept answers where children have attempted to work out how much each type of sweet costs per 100 g.

Page 6
Planning a party
1. 24 children (21 friends, 2 brothers of a friend and yourself)
2. 3 packs
   £4.47
3. 8 packs
   1 ball

Page 7
4. 6 packs
   1,000 ml (accept: 1 litre)
5. 3 tables
   0 spaces
6. 18 chairs
   yes
   42 − 18 = 24 (the number of children at the party)

Page 8
7. 1 hour
   $1\frac{1}{2}$ hours
   $4\frac{1}{2}$ hours
   £45
8. £36
   1 hour 30 minutes
9. £96
   £86

Page 9
10. 8 prizes
    50p
    bubbles 150 ml (49p)
    Accept a correct calculation based on an incorrect answer (an answer other than 50p) to the first part.
11. whistle (2p), toy plane (5p), fake moustache (4p), yoyo (3p) whistle (2p)
    Check your child's answer is based mathematically (e.g. they have the lowest price)

Page 10
Going camping
1. 870 cm
   Check that a horizontal line of symmetry is drawn that divides the tent into two matching halves.
   parallel

Page 11
2. £26
   £2.50
3. yes
   40 minutes after 3:30 pm is 4:10 pm, so there is still 10 minutes before the tractor ride at 4:20 pm.
   yes
   Archery is 30 minutes long so will finish at 6:30 pm. The last tractor ride is 6:40 pm, so there will be 10 minutes to spare.

Page 12
Decorating a bedroom
1. $12 \, m^2$
   4 tins
   £34
   £39.60
   £5.60

Page 13
2. £260
   £35
   desk

Page 14
3. $48 \, m^2$
   $40 \, m^2$

Page 15
4. £200
   £38
   Accept correct calculations based on an incorrect area (an area other than $48 \, m^2$).
   plain deep pile, plain short pile, two-tone short pile

Page 16
Visiting a library
1. 21 days
   23rd January
2. 60, 60, 90, 80, 110, 160
   547 books
   550 books
   500 books

Page 17
3. 46 cm, 70 cm, 60 cm
   64 cm, 66 cm
4.

Book	Number of pages	To the nearest ten	To the nearest hundred
1	109	110	100
2	356	360	400
3	274	270	300
4	351	350	400
5	101	100	100

   1,191 pages
   1,190 pages
   1,200 pages
   1,000 pages

Page 18
Flying on holiday
1. quarter to 2 in the afternoon / pm
   12:00
2. 132 passengers
   1,188 passengers

Page 19
3. 12 suitcases
   693 g
4. 17 days
5. 5,428 flights
   6,418 flights